Dying Old and Dying Young

Dying Old and Dying Young

poems by

Susan Williams

with photographs by
Sharon Scapple, Garret Williams,
and others

Minnesota Voices Project Number 31

NEW RIVERS PRESS 1987

Grateful acknowledgement is made to the editors of the following publications in which some of these poems first appeared: *Calliope, Earth's Daughters, Fall-Out, Inkling Anthology, Labyris, Loonfeather, Sing, Heavenly Muse, Undercurrents,* and others.

Dying Old and Dying Young has been made possible by grants from the Jerome Foundation, the Dayton Hudson Foundation (with funds provided by B. Dalton, Bookseller), the First Bank System Foundation, and the National Endowment for the Arts (with funds appropriated by the Congress of the United States).

New Rivers Press books are distributed by:

The Talman Company	and	Bookslinger
150 - 5th Avenue		213 E. 4th St.
New York, NY 10011		St. Paul, MN 55101

Dying Old and Dying Young has been manufactured in the United States of America for New Rivers Press, Inc. (C.W. Truesdale, editor/publisher), 1602 Selby Ave., St. Paul, MN 55104 in a first edition of 1,200 copies.

For Lola Hardy Sandretzky
(1853-1887)

and

Maren Hartz Evenson
(1864-1954)

and

For my Mother and Father
Marjorie Foels Evenson

and

Oswald Sunde Evenson

Table of Contents

III. Threading the Needle

I.

Motherweave: Witnesses

"Would it not rather be proof of our own irremediable poverty if we should permit the dead to die?"

Natalie Barney

Lola, Delosia Jane

(from a daguerreotype, August 1868)

Straight-faced as a soldier boy
in the grave holding eye,
half her life
burned away
that August afternoon.

What she saw.
What she knew.

> Don't move now.
> Slow exposure.

What the grass has grown over, beautiful,
emphatic as she was.

Motherweave

I see you in dreams
    in a room
    in a circle
    together
    piecing a quilt.
Your names braided into your talk:

    Ella, Anna
    Johanne
    Wilhelmina
    Delosia Jane
    Maren Kristine
    Matelon
    Krista
    Julianne, Alianne
    Ellerine
    Susan
    Susie Rose

Dream myself into your names of
women long dead, rubbed smooth
from the inside as
talk between sisters
stitching a revery
talking
a quilt.

Dying Old and Dying Young

In the picture
they sit
almost touching
forever
married
straight
as spring rain
as corn rows
as knives in the drawer.

She is the second sister he married.
They buried the first in bridesdress forever
embracing her baby. Her picture
hung in the front room
fifty-two years
faced the rocker.

Rocked
in all seasons, locked
in the blinkless line of her eye,
startled
forever.

The Obligation to be Beautiful

"Don't cry baby," her father would say. "You're not pretty when you cry."

Great-grandma took arsenic,
just a pinch in her chamomile tea
to keep that pallid cast in her cheek
her husband loved. He married her
for her lovely ethereal look (like an angel
he said), but now and again
sent a wandering glance
after a face in the street just as wan and pale.

Now and again she stirred in
a ghostly pinch. Said it was nothing
to her whalebone stays. Made her a little bit giddy
was all. She was fresh as a lily for nearly six years.

Old woman leaves her home, remembers another remove

I didn't want want to go.
Did all I could to sway him but he was restless, nothing would do
but we must go West. To Oregon.

We started when the mud was hard, in April, from St. Joe
with forty Conestoga wagons, prairie schooners. Will and me, Ma
and Pa, Ella, Sam, the twins, Ida, Arianne. The baby was born
along the way. My cousin Charlie rode with us on horseback
the first day — fourteen miles.

Started on an ill omen to my mind when a bride with a party
from Ohio was struck by a loose bullet as they chivareed her
the night before we set out and died next day.

We had three new-married couples with us. This was to be, so to say,
their honeymoon, a lark, two thousand miles. That meant as little to me then as
twenty thousand or a million. One of the brides, from Strawberry Point Iowa,
pretty as spring, said to Ma, "How many girls have had
such a wedding tour?"

Third day out we passed a fresh grave, just past the Sweetwater,
bent wagon iron for headstone.
It was dug full of holes.
I held Ida tight. She had no more idea of things than the chicks
we had lashed to the sides in crates. She or Anna either one, playing
tag in the long grass, berrying all day a mild day, fishing the rivers.
Only nights sometimes they scared themselves with Indians, or a coyote
shrieked and cracked our sleep and then they hollered out to Will to
build the fire higher.

The Indians never meddled with us, though we heard the Sioux were burning
grass to the north to turn back wagons with cattle. They took
what got left by the way — heavy mirrors and picture frames, dressers,
rockers, what-nots, a Dutch oven we saw one day but you can't call that
stealing. We heard they stole children but I never knew it to happen
for certain. Mid-summer Nelda Kellogg from two wagons back — they were
from Rock County Illinois — wandered off as we waited to cross
the Burning River. The Cayuse traded her to a smith in the train behind us
for a milk cow and a feather tick. Her folks had her back in three weeks
time. In that time, often as not walking in sand past our ankles,

16

we passed eighty-eight graves between the Burning and Devil's Gate.
Alma Kellogg counted them. I counted trees. We were luck-mocked
Alma said. Her milk dried up and the chug chug of the wheels those weeks
liked to make her mad she said, as if they chugged her baby's name
over and over. She looked half mad with her wild red hair.

The Cayuse dug up graves for shirts and in that way spread cholera.
When Pa died we dug him deep in the road and let the oxen tramp the grave
so none could dig him up for his clothes, which we had burned. We buried
the baby under a willow and piled on rocks and picketed the grave
to keep the wolves off. They tore up the raft and walking plow
to make pickets. I wouldn't get in the wagon till the men had done it,
though we lost half a day by it. I only half cared if they had left me,
which they knew and they did it. I left a note on the twisted pitchfork
marker to passers to please keep up for Jesus' sake my baby's grave.
It seemed hard to leave her alone like that and never go back. If only
we had a picture Ida said. It was grave-scarred country
all the way to Oregon.

Dear Sister

We have sailed in the belly of the boat forty days. Night
gathers in the sails. I fold and unfold your letters, I
do better than some. Sedda Lengstrom from Lillestad parish
has forgotten how to sleep. Her eyes roll in her head she
can't stop talking. Her baby in a sheet in the cold sea.

    "A tree must be bound.
    A dirty fire won't burn.
    Bees won't stay with a thief."

Still as a candle stands slips her thin hands along my belly;
so skinny she has lost her milk already. Says in my ear
in a drowning voice, "No place is home
till children are born there." I swell and sway like a ship.
Try to keep lice off the twins. Read by a lurchy flame and write
by the moon. One forenoon we passed a ship from home, a high country
pine lashed to its mast. The sea wears you down like fire.
The English sailors don't bother me — louts — they shout and think
we must understand.

"English hurts my teeth," you say. I read your letters every day.
Woke in the storehouse loft this morning again, the two of us
braided together, barley and hay, fermenting beer, apples in the
snapping air. Smuggled giggles under the quilt. "A tree not bound
with straw won't bear fruit," Sedda says. She is surely mad. I remember
everything she says. I try to picture you stretching sheets over the lilacs
to dry in that treeless land. Lying among the cows for company; watching
the copper sky for tornadoes. Heat that pulls wolves out of the hills
to fight with the dogs in the chickenyard. Snow drifted over the fences
forever. Over the window. What a country for weather that must be!

Your fire letter twists in me — waking to red light like hellfire boiling
the greased paper window. All through that red night waiting, fire coming,
leaping rivers eating the prairie, coming. How you set a backfire
against it and went out to meet it with wet feedsacks, missing a step
in your sleep. Dream of you lost in that hard country, waiting
for your body to betray you again. So hard to think of nameless farms
miles apart — surely not Norwegian miles. And who will come
when your time comes, sister?

Met the conjurewoman the morning we left, witching for water, eyes
like dried blood, twitched her twist of a stick at me, took my hands,
"light as wrens," hoarse as a crow; squeezing a vinegar sponge
from her sack "It's a sin to take a child from his father." A sin.
A tick beneath the skin.

The birds watched us leaving. The lindens were grieving. But the land,
seven years, grudged us a living. Fed Einar's spite. Nothing would do
but we must go to America. Off from those Old Country knots. Never
to see Mother's face, or that other we never name. Never to sit on the graves.

Fiddlers led us out of the chapel's blossoming walls, three times around
the wooden lace houses, circling the fields, the mustard was waving.
Silver bride's crown weaving into my hair. Carrying a small bouquet
of fear. That old woman told me — but no one thought not to marry
in Hitterdahl. Marriage knotted the village together. And Einar
must have me — wouldn't let me be (you remember). So I pieced my
thirteenth quilt.

Candlestick pattern. Lemon and cinnamon, bleedingheart red you could read
for a mile in the sun. Next winter made a cold bed of evergreen. Branches
and linen. Watched the woodcarver's thin hands bless the linden, pale
on the larch, the copper beech coffin. Is this the same moon

that walks on tall legs in the Stavanger mountain? Dark
with the faces of trolls? Love took me
like the moon takes the sea. Ticked with the buried heart, night
gathered in the trees, kissed the trunks kissed the leaves. Seed
of pale wood sailing, waiting to blossom.

In the mountains spring is a shower of mornings — chokecherries
cloudberries waterfalls stitching the hills. Horses loose
in the high country spring took me, high and sad
as a Hardanger fiddle. Do they have this moon in America too? Mad
as a woman come out of the mountain. We met one last time
at the foot of the braided tree watched by the horses and ginger goats
love carved me. Heard the old heart's mad voice.

"How did the troll see to polish his only eye?" Sedda asks. I can't tell
her. Her eyes burn my skin. I slip in a crack in her fever again.

Finally ran out of the fog after three days, today
light sucks color out of the sky. One sour cloud overhead, one
seed of wood. Weep for the sheeted, the unshadowed dead. Heard
a heart beat my wrist in my head. (Whose body is this? Whose
sloping belly?) Evil multiples
out of the old mystery.

Kiss Krista for me.
My namesake.

Such a hard crossing.
We all paid the cost.
Our children will pay for a hundred years.

They say we will reach America soon. With these words I kiss you
a hundred times.

Maren Hartz (1864-1954)

How you crossed in winter with a letter,
"This Christian family," wrote the Sogneprest, "well known to me,
the father, a farmer, is born, baptized, confirmed, married
in Hitterdahl parish. . . . "

Mother with child, father, the twins, one blind, all seasick
but you
up at first light
unlaced from the past
watching for aspen, dreaming
of norns, of cloudberries.

How you carried water to the picketed willow,
the one they left standing,
past the braided fields
the air was snapping.

How you brazened it out when the doctor didn't come that Christmas,
"You must take more lefse — one more helping. "
Took the knife when they left and Ida
the oldest
pushed the oak trunk to the door
kneeled by the bed
the two of you,
then winter tightened on you.

Ragged your hands till they bled till pus ran between your fingers
years later
the children fought over the homeplace

Depression
and who should have it.

You wanted a long slow death,
surrounded, medieval
and almost got it
old woman
under an old tree
in a flowered dress
in summer
sun spills along the branches
splits the gillyflowers
patches the ground at your feet,
wind lifts the corner of your dress
in the picture
tips its shadow into the tree,
afternoon shadows, woman and tree
run around you and frame you,
rain hangs in the air, never moving
you stand
tree straight
in the sun
in the shade
under the lightning-struck oak.

Susie Rose

In her mother's house
    her voice skipped up the steps ahead of her
    laugh splashed rain fragrant fruit-of-the-rose slow-kissed
    the roots awake, woke
    rose-rinsed mornings curving into life,
she never had the habit of grief.
    Her awkward beauty struck like light, hair dressed high to sit
    and think
    of peaches in a silver bowl, eyes (will be the last to die)
    set straight in her face as the hawk falls.

Years circle.

A shark in her husband's house.

The old (Mother was always up at first sun)
thin-lidded
are early wakers:
something wears away beneath the skin rose-veined
in the weak winter light
loosening
her ragged words arrive
after her lips move, too long
she looks at the sound
and beyond
her own voice makes,
turns her face away, the mirror erases all but fierce eyes

body falls away
the leaves let go.

Still, violets bloom in the winter room that wouldn't bloom
in any room or season,
blossoms like bruises at the window.

Shark in the house she was
a proper shark for housework.

This riddle moves too slow for me to catch it.

Mattie

Every Sunday we went to Grandpa's
Once a month to town.

Shades up shades down,
turn the violets around,
plant pick bake scrape

Old men outlive all love,
Life repeats itself.

Break stir fold scrape cut a snake with a hoe,
she scared me so.
Babies lept out of her all mixed up like
a braided rug. I chopped
as many as I could.

Polished the chest with salt and oil.
He went to church to hire threshers.
Set the Blue Willow china behind glass.
Preacher came out of the wall, made a circle.
It does feel fine to have things in their place.

Little ones braided in bed every night they giggled
all day. Up the steps down, some mornings early
I follow my breath
all through my body. Life burned high,
he was handsome that autumn, his beard
came in red, dashing as thieves.

Leaves leave the willow in early September, one
each day, sweet to breathe the leafy air. Remember
the moon from a high open place,
the cat-caught mole at my feet.

Set the table clear the table (Can my hands breathe
underwater?) food in a circle they feed on the food
of my blood, this heart hates a late beat I tasted
my own sweet blood in the tub. November

is pig-killing. (Move the violets away from the window.)
We keep the cream in a crock in the cellar
and crocks of lard.

Milk strain skim drain
wind the clock rock with the clock, in winter
you can't tell the dead from the living. Whose hands
were awake? How long do dead trees stand? What grows
in the dark? Why won't it stop? Won't speed up? Who

is the woman who rises up in that chiming room?
Walks out the clock? Walks
to the fat white cattails that shine the night? Building
a quilt of light. What's coiled on that plate? Why
wait for morning? Why
do we wait?

Without the plates the table would fly away. "Next
we'll have gypsies in the henhouse, " he said one day.
Does often seem as if life's someplace else. A road
connects towns, finally cities. Who are those polished city women? What
do cities know? Who set the violets
so close to the window?

Up the steps down to the henhouse, watch
so you don't slip
catching a skittery Saturday pullet, twisting
her head around. Every Sunday

sit up to the table, spiders spin out of themselves
in a circle. They must have put a secret sign on the door
he said, "No one else gets so many tramps. " I dreamt

my tablecloth stretched to heaven.
So white it was.

Mission Circle meets once a month, they
could have surprised me any day, my house
was that clean.

Forty generations of corn and beans.
Take them to town, don't forget
my egg money.

Wheat from dead bellies, corn out of corpses
all swelled up
swelling to heaven. I watched his barn burn, bellying out,
breathing fast, smoke
circled over the house, something laughed
a heaving laugh. Then I heard
the heifer scream.

Month when the sun uncovers the ground again,
that's a good day.
I wrote in my daybook
the weather each day. Sleep outside
when you can't sleep Ma used to say. Sleep by the creek
by a gypsy fire. Suck a stone if you're thirsty
and can't get to water. You can't
train raspberries, sweetgrass
won't grow in rows.

Nelda across the road has broken eyes,
runny as eggs.
Should go see her now the road's open.
Works her jaw back and forth when she talks, my hair
gives off an animal smell in summer
walking, picking butter-and-eggs, her head twists around,
her eyes are circles. She gives me mushrooms, says to eat them
the same day or turn into toadstools. So deep in that thought
I forgot to breathe. Snakes hunt underground, gypsies
have circus wrists and ankles. Can my hands breathe?
That round of birthdays comes round again.

Dreamt of Ma
dead in the birthbed, drowned in blood, her sisters
around in a ring — they were seven. Words in a circle
he killed the willow to make more field.
"Soon I can reach out my kitchen window and pick corn" I said.
"That'll be a saving" he said, blowing smoke rings, its trunk
was a hundred circles,
I counted.

Ring
around
the last rose of summer I never
let the girls play by the creek
or go near the flowing well.

Nelda

First life together.
You were my father.
Smothered my waking face, "Don't
wake your mother. " Rust in your voice (trying to listen past).
"Devil," you said, twisting my legs apart. Blood
in the bed. Who washed those sheets?

     She's clumsy, that one.
     All bumps and bruises. Broody. No wonder
     she makes her father mad. Screaming
     the house awake. Eyes too sad to look at
     more than a minute.

Click of the lock. Throat snapped shut. My face
came unhooked. Eyes like dead weather. Said
I was crazy. Couldn't stop screaming. Birds
frozen to the trees. Rats in the walls, chirping, words
I'd never said. Never heard. Turn

like a key. Over my shoulder. Another room. Moon
was a bruise on the night. Threw her head
from side to side. Drew up her legs and died with no word.
Strangled sheets. Pa
wouldn't let me be.
You again. Me.
Caught me alone in the pasture one day. Under
the slash pine. Heard the birds saying
a storm was coming. Swallow flew into a big-bellied cloud.
Knocked the dog into the creek — ragged breathing. Not enough time
to scream under those drowning sounds. Telling each other
what your hands undid. Pine needles in my hair. Let the dog chew
on my toes in the rain to feel if I can feel again. Another time.

Brother with your razor face. Another place. Busted nests. Voice
split the air. Twisted roots and twisted branches. Water
rushing in my ear. Birds can't fly if their wings get wet.
Made a fist around my wrist. "Kiss your dirty elbow
and turn into a sparrow. " Turn.

Same key, Another name — husband.
Now husband (how did it happen?).
Million-eyed skin. You in my sleep again. (Sure as breath
we return.) You in the morning. Smearing the air. Prying
me out of a dream of sleep. Dreaming

a swallow asleep in the wind. Dreaming the summer
I learned how to swim in my body, before
it betrayed me. Dreaming the light
I swallowed.

Ella

He was a good man
still
it nearly killed me to give up teaching
though the big boys were bullies,
big as bulls some of them and knew I was timid (shy
is too timid of a word). I was plain
and all the men handsome in that family, fancy
dancers and married plain women, though I wasn't homely.

We got a place a mile from the homeplace, eighty acres.
The babies came, six in eight years
and pork 3 cents a pound and milk cheap as dirt.
Saturdays we took our eggs to town, never sure
we had enough for what we needed, not to mention
a bag of apples or peppermint candy.
It sometimes seemed we were luck-mocked
week to week, though others were worse off.
I tried not to get too blue.
My sister Solveig — she was the beauty — they found her
wandering
in a housedress in a snowfield along the three-rutted road
where Lindahl's path crosses the Bath Road that goes to town,
out of her head, talking to trolls
she said.

I tried to read a book a week, then one a month then
Nordisk Folkeblad when it came out. I took Mrs. Browning
out of the trunk in the spring and sat down
if no meals got made that day. The day they took his cows
for TB that night late he broke my dream apart
with his singing. He was leveling hay and singing
one of the old songs when I slid the door open. "English
is no tongue to sing in," he said, "or swear or tell stories
or love in, *kjaere*. English is to count in."

He wore red suspenders like Pa's and I wept
for his discouraged shoulders.

33

Oscar

You look good I say.
I always did he says.
Rocked me till he fell asleep, Grandma laughed when she found us,
book in my hands
thirty years ago
after haying all day.

Now it's winter outside the window,
white in and out.
Did the lake crack last night? You have a nice view.
See
the lake's frozen over.

He looks at the bag. Not the one
his father wore for fourteen years and smoked White Owl stogies
to hide the smell.
Not the one he expected,
went out to level hay while Grandma slept
expecting.

      We had house parties in those days. All night.
      Many's the house would hold. They'd push the chairs
      out of the front room and roll up the rug. Haul
      the stove out under the trees to make more room.
      Sometimes I went and Ella stayed home. She couldn't
      dance all night like I could.

      She was a good one you know. We were the first
      to sit together in church. Before that the men
      sat on the pulpit side and women and children
      on the baptism side. Women would sit with four or
      five squirming kids. After I and Ella sat together
      others did too.

He worked to pay for Ole, she said.
Paid the Mayo doctors.
Depression years.
Eight thousand dollars.

We used to get some bad food haying. I'd stuff it
in my pockets and give it to the dogs and they'd say
'What have you got for the dogs today Oscar?' I remember
an angel food so thick with flies you couldn't see
a speck of cake. That was on Selmer Amley's place.

Pa got bit by a mud turtle on Amley's creek. He always
limped after that. Couldn't catch us. We'd play the fool
and run and he'd holler Norwegian after us.

Called him when their dogs went mad or heifers' bellies swelled or
calves breached. They said he should have been a vet.

Something bad is happening he says.
Where did they hide my wallet?
They're coming after my cows.

That August afternoon
stitching fences
grasshoppers snapping in the tall grass
wind blew up ice
out of the north
so cold it hurt to swallow.
Hitched his shoulder into the wind
tucked his chin into his throat
walked his loose-as-water high-hipped roll into his breath
followed it home
shouldering into the cold snow
to find them that way.

Just that fast it happened.

Something bad he says in a whisper like silk ripping.
They're coming to haul them away.
Up North.
They say they have TB.

It's all right I say. Look
how the lake is frozen

Barn swallows

swooped us on the way to the barn
after supper in summer
looped through their own almond strokes
made last year, shapely,
peach-bellied.

You could reach up and grab one Grandpa
said and reached up but
they wouldn't like it.

A dream ago

a hand was writing
wrote
raised letters
in the broken dark,
wrote on foam,

a one-winged bird was swimming
in and out of sleep,
skating the white lake.

Night the moon followed me home,
turned when I turned, waited
outside my window,
subtle abductor. Night

my dream took a wrong turn,
left me behind
in revery,
sleepwalker
in an unfinished childhood.

For Grandpa and Grandma and Gaston Bachelard

I. Buttoned in a clovey cupboard
    dreamer of lavender drawers
    me in my house of a hundred hollows inhaling the day from the
    fruitcellar rootcellar sweet
    hole inhabitant happily cornered under the hood of the woodpile hunched
    in the hunchback porch among almonds
    reading the day
    immured in the desk's secret heart away thought unfolds
    in the windowseat steamertrunk steep spicy closet closing
    in daydreams unrolls in the walnutbin deep-breathing
    wardrobe false-bottom cinnamon
    chest.

II. Follow the swallow into her nest
    the owl to his hollow,
    the otter slides over the pumpstream
    unfathomed
    spaniel sleeps under the house (How far her lair goes no one knows
    nor what she becomes in the slow heart of night) under
    my house of a hundred hollows.

III. The world came to live in me in my house in me in my
    house of dark dreaming
    stars ago.

    The well flowed into the cellar, taking no candle.

    Aloneness had a top and bottom there

    then

    a hundred centers
    revery no sides.

The old woman's mother comes for her

Worms can't have me yet.
Not while I see some light. See her
blooming as morning, taking the horses molasses, taking
the path past the river ran silver in spring with new water she stepped
step by stone, over the river,
the almost-ghost in the grass. So long

you've been gone.
See the birthbed, billowing red gown of hair on a white pillow,
birthstar marching
down your bare arm. Waltzed by when I fussed you and Pa
grabbed me didn't miss a beat two three
hats on the bed
bat in the kitchen. It was all bad Aunt Cat said, called me
by my longer name. "Gypsies in the henhouse, tramps at the door.
This farm's a carnival!" razory shoulders, eyes
like hard weather, she put dead things on the table, I wouldn't
eat. "Plant by a new moon, plant to a wild tune
in your head" you said "Watch for wasps buried in crabapples,
wish on them. Wish on snow geese twice a year, wishbone scratched
on the sky — hear them tuning up? Some snakes hunt underground,
you can tell time by a dandelion, slap your chest twice
to keep off the cold and dance when you're sad."
"All bad."

"Eyes need trees, a certain number to sleep. This willow
will watch over me when I'm dead, and the black oak," you said.

Thanksgiving
you scratched my back
right at the table where it itched, your wrist smelled vanilla.
Cousins and uncles — "Such a big girl to be Mama's baby" — my face
in your sagey lap. "I've spoiled all my girls — would again. Ma
spoiled me. Look how good I've turned out!" smelling vanilla.
"But don't they have gallant hair, my daughters? Mad-red as blarney
you'd think we were Irish." Rocked back on your heels, lash shadows
on your cheek under the evergreen tilted your head back and laughed
at the gypsy who read death in chickens' guts:
        Step over the mother crack don't break
        your mother's lovely long back.

Rag-curled our hair
Saturday nights filled the tub five times from the pump,
saved rainwater, hands in the dishwater drowning — who are you? So white
in the room with the cabbage rose walls. Gasping for light. Hands
laced my neck — "Don't let me drown" in a low drowning voice.

Two miles to school when the river froze over. "Here comes your mother
with hot potatoes. The idea!" Your face gave the world back, then
your eyes went away. Pulled out Nell's glass eye, hid it away in your
waxy white collar. No one saw. Then I was my own witness, hear that tune?

The wild one we planted to under the planting plum moon
coming for me — step two three too fast to dance to she
comes through a tunnel of mustard up past the old horse path. Now I remember —
her wrist tasted almond.

"Mine is the voice that calls from inside the light." See you I
hear you softsinging me swinging me waltzing me flinging me lifting me laughing
me lilting me lighting me
home again
home.

II.

Survival by Accident

*"Beginnings are always delightful;
the threshold is the place to pause."*

Goethe

Morning

Say it's morning.
Say I'm coming.
Say the hummingbirds are humming.
Say the trees and leaves are raining
Ropes of water
Slow returning.
Say my wrists and throat are burning
Bleeding ruby on the morning.
Say the birds are bubbling up.
Pearl-bellied swallows blooming   pear
and willow
Plum tree turning

Say it's morning.
Say I'm coming.

We would look up

from our books
at the same time
you'd say
set up your fears in rows like bowling pins,
I'll tumble them down.
I'd say tell me (I'll tell you mine) your tender adventures all
night in words that fling their arms around me like wild cucumber vines.
Marry me to this moment.
Slip that riggish grin into my sleep.
Let me be the one to start that smile
every morning
I will be a garden
sprouting, flowering
every morning thornapple purple milkweed seagrapes snow crocus
roseberry
petaled together,
you in the garden.

What more to say about clouds — only that they would bloom in
rows outside our window
slow as Cezanne
from our fluted and tuliped black pineapple gingerbread bed

we would look up.

Woke in the night

Woke in the night to walk with me down
beside the dark creek to smell the wet lilacs
to hear the pines hum. The doe's eye blooms
in the fawn and is gone. Summer is gone.
Fall falls away. The moon
is loose in your eye and you
begin again to kiss my hair, my hip
where it begins to curve
your hand
reprints itself behind my eyes as I
begin again to come at last as night
assembles — all the seasons of the moon —
home. The pines hum,

drunk with perfume it was dark
going down to the creek.

Summer Lake

One
then another
loved me one summer,
one hand slid along my side in the dark riverwater   parted
my Highland hair whispered my lips alive
under the water
I kissed the winey bruise on his side a fish
kissed my wrist,
followed a vein to its end I
hummed to his perfect pitch, watching
the other
smile bit his lip,
child in a room with a corpse
in that deep unmade house.

    I kissed first
    that lush and starry pulse — mind stumbles back.
    That place.

    Ducks asleep on the summer shore   beaks ducked deep
    in their own duck-fluff,
    we swam like ghosts so not to wake them, dove
    like things in the mirror   the wind
    blew hot blew cold the same moment
    rained on the dark-eyed pines
    rained all around the lake   you
    kissed my pulse awake   "Grandma! Grandma!"

    left in the churchyard
    rice powder on your face
    grave grass grown over
    seven stones in a row.

That night we couldn't sleep the wind was so exciting.
Blew the birds into song,
wild scoop of cloud scooped down.

How far from star to star?
Do the stairs go up or down?

Heloise behind the wall the wind is at the window.

Uncle Daniel danced with lightning
in the thigh-high grass
and lived

between the barn and silo

laugh cracks the night — whose?
Who's awake? Across the lake
laughing? "He was always stormy-minded"
heard Aunt Cass say "Once
I have a passion for a man
he's the one." Who was with her?

Torn blouse. Tears in her voice her
asking breasts, Grandma's wax face.
All her stories ghost stories told by the light
of a long-dead star. The ground
will open for us somewhere
but not this summer   lavender

in Grandma's chest, camphor, Grandpa's charleyhorse.
Bone gone wrong in the toe he said. Can't fish the lake
till the bodies come up. "Thistles
in the summer wheat
from what they did last Christmas." Hired man.
Lost his luck. What does he mean?

Uncle Justin sneaked snakes into church to hear them sing.
Dead in Dakota with no letter.

Pale Greek lovers between pale columns
lemon-cool in the cool west bedroom the boy
bends over the girl's bent knee, she
shades her face from his milky skin flecked with sun
cloud cities drowned cities twin cities sleep
in the ivory mountains stringing
a shrunken eye of a lake, shush
of sun in the pines hissing
rain
waits
in the willow a minute,
then moves on,
follows the blue-hills into the lemon light
down past the cow pasture child in the grass fast asleep.

Let's marry under this tree! Marry me
to a tree bleeding secrets steep as the bottomless place
in the lake. Won't forgive Grandpa for killing the willow
to make more field
in May
we lived close to the lilac's breath   twirled
till we dropped in a deep-breathing heap,
hummingbirds danced for us faster faster!
But this is July. Lemon lilies
in the west bedroom, rose leaves alive on a polished table,
someone's mother in the window
baby snakes braid out a bloody mother
mowed over
knotted blood, savage tribe, skipping stones, old crone
eyes like dried blood
someone, hands knotted, one pillared window;
those stones are babies, rose petals, dead
in the birthbed
bled seven days they couldn't stop it. Mother.
Is this blood a baby? The bathwater's bleeding let's
marry in water! Run your tongue over those words while I bleed
to death Romans
opened their veins in the bath. Ivanhoe, read me from Ivanhoe
from the window while I bleed

secret as shade, summer bride somewhere
lost in the shuttered house, August   dust danced past
now kiss my pulse awake
ankle my wrist burst out singing my skin
answers spilling each other,
each other's secret — that lake starts underground
in the next county — float
in the hammock all drifting afternoon strung
stone deaf between redheaded trees "Let's go
berrying!" stained in the spongy woods sun stumbles after us
"Put your ear on the ground, hear it? Water
trapped underground. " Dead babies
when cousins marry,
put your hands on me
blinkless as kittens.
Whose cat-tan eyes?
Whose face in the branches?
"Hurry up slowpokes. The sun's going down."

Tucked in a dim in a twin constellation asleep
on the sleeping porch all but us
reading
along the cool shelves found a bookmark,
brown tintype child in a box buried
finally
under the high elm
in Grandma's jewel casket.
Over the lake milky skeleton of night looping
hands in the water
opened
my thready legs "Blood" that voice split apart
"I'm bleeding!" mixed up
in seaweed we made first milk.

Blood and milk.
What does it make?

"Cut more lemons, fetch the ice chunk from the well, don't
fall in now — no nonsense! Put sunhats on. The idea!

You'll burn again.
Won't sleep for burning skin."
"You twins you two? Wasn't here in March was you?
Miz Hardy dead? Went fast. Did she leave word
for the Watkins man?"

Promised
a child
no matter
where I go
throw my smile cast my laugh fling my love very
love flies
like a duck like a goose
like a nightfloating ghost,
a nightsinging lark like a lake-haunting fish-hunting hawk
back to you
in the bulb cellar blooming from the wrist.

You didn't leave word for me, listen — hear?
There's a mushrat down here.

Kissed in that sleepy room kissed
our dreams into bloom, lake bloomed where we touched dark
garden far to reach kissed
in the blind water knotted
our blood forever.

Plowing up stars

in a page of rain
afternoon
after the others left,
wrote on each other's bodies:
DREAM we wrote
DREAM
on our foreheads and fell
asleep.
Ships in a bottle,
flinging in space.

What is it you want

when you come at me like that
breathing me in like a cat?
And I am a chapel of grass, of mint
in landscape crisp to breaking

you breathless, gulping,
your needy eyes on me,
your slow bruising eyes
and hands slide down my sides.

Tell me in my ear
then everywhere.

That afternoon

dancing
that long dance we danced our bodies
forgot to be grave.
You sat in the small of your back in the corner laughing
that wildsoft laugh.
Your mouth is a flower in the rain
you said
a snail in the brain,
and you are a chapel of grain in the wind,
winding
waiting
dancing down pain,
deeper
deeper
a fire in the rain,
deeper
deeper
past the gatekeeper
again
again
again.

It was exactly October

late afternoon I was
homesick for old trees,
the smell of bruised apples, wet leaves
and your neck.
Then you were there
in the door,
looked past the others
walked in with no word,
eyes
set straight in your face, your shoulders
wanton, broke
the light's perfect circle, rolled
to slow pleasure
under your coat where I touched you
exactly.

The face of a man

The face of a man untouched
as a boy, his slow hands, the way
he stands at the window, the measured gesture,
weighed down with waiting, that cold perfume.

Blue rhythm at the wrist, dull eyes the tight lip
the chill
beneath
the chilly skin. Thinking

the things I made him do
one pale afternoon half past shame. I

look at him where I touched him and touching
his crumbling lip I kiss
past the loose pulse dissolving wrist kiss
where he touched me slow
in the window never looking
at my face.

You catch me

looking at you as you turn
to watch me
swinging my feet to the beat of your heart in the dark I say
"Let's think of tracks buried under the city, the weather
under the water. " You lie
silent as fish
as eggs in a dish. I tell you that beavers and porcupines
move through the city by river. Once you said truth's
the thing the body tells; showed me a secret way
out of my skin.
"Let's do something clean — learn a new language, translate
a dream, " I say
"walk a rope over a deep slippery river through clouds
the color of apricot jelly. "

I tell you a dream that explains everything
but you are playing chess in your head.

Keepsake

You spoke.
You broke it.
I was reading, said
if no one speaks (and I won't speak) before
I read one page we're safe: you
me
a fire between us,
easy as cats in my body
improbable, you
unrepeatable,
looking the way a man looks. When

I was the secret bride of the city
thought I would always be
at the center, then
followed fear around in a circle,
hope's slow widow
but not so old; he
looked at me
the way a man looks whose dreams break apart on your
arm, your wrist, your luminous neck, the places
a cat likes to be, we together.

> beauty
> he thought
> only he thought
> was beauty,
> bent over roses
> bent into clover
> "bent my knee to beauty
> as she bent to me"

One yes between me and life
and I said it
so keep it
for my sake
the ache, a keepsake.

And you said, too soon, before
I could turn I have something
one thing
to say.

Laura

The beautiful name of my husband's friend Laura.
Sends us wild honey from Colorado.
Gold mountain honey with a funny note.
Sends my son all three bears for his birthday.
Steals into town in buzzing summer to leave her name
in the dust of our dashboard.
　Who's been sitting, eating, writing in my front seat,
smiling, laughing? Funny
how silence arranges itself in a grinning sentence
under the hot locust buzz of the scrubgrass.

Remember the sky
when it was so bright it hurt?
We saw the red deer at the door, a family
safe inside winter
that longasleep nerve
under the yeasty moon woke like fragrant bread in my belly.

Farther than farthest-down fear you are in me.
Open my skin, exhausted border, first to cross, last intruder,
last to utter the warm name of winter. (Who left
and left the scented loaf?)

Funny how silence arranges itself around a honeyed blade of a name, love
comes around a sour corner, blood runs to the heart
giving what can't be bought, beautiful
hibernate name, remember? The places we went? The things we said?
The scented bread? How blood broke out
under the skin one winter. Now silence like cat eyes
caught in the headlights.
We sigh in code, slow blade between us, slow-circle the truth,
start back from that stinging name.

Who will unfasten this twitching ghost?
Who will love a woman's anger?

Latches his seatbelt, a promise
to Laura.

The moon the mad moon

when it lept into bed with me, fell in my dream,
swelled like a stemmed vein just missed
my last pulse, big-mouthed as a bell; scarlet
as bull's blood it knelt dark and red
by the side of the bed, said
"What do you call
your tongue in the moon?" spilled its tongue in the gleaming
scoop of my throat; then I missed a step, came out of sleep
with its name on my lips then it straddled my hips tried to ride
bloody galloping thunder
astride the nightmare
echoes knocked at the walls
crawly shadows crawled out
stars shot from my wrists
constellations and ghosts
of last year's lost pulse I lay
noseless as death,
silent and pale as a fish in a cold lake it
hooked itself full in me
bloomed like a rooster a blister like grace unzipped
out of a cloud bloody wide as a city the great sucky moon came unstuck
crooked-backed and it took a last run at me
planted its nose in me
rose like a gold yeasty loaf again
crept in me lept in me slept in me wouldn't go home and you

never knew
beside me looped over me your arm around me
like some crescent moon.

Married

In the passionate gloom of that darkening room we danced
that slow dance in the curve of the moon till he saw
in the shadows melting the wall the tilt
of our shoulders our hips lift and fall. Reading
my lips though the back of your head: "Since he wants
never to see me again, he won't let me go."
"New lock on an old door." "Old wine
in new bottles, " laughing off key, pouring a whiskey. Eyes
would not release my face, your voice
lifting into a question.
Old tree groans twice in the frozen wind for answer, your breath
turns around inside mine.   We are married

for all those deeper lies than love, the three of us,
braided together. Trapped in that wisdom we shivered into
one lingering winter, love starved down to waiting.

The lake cracks. A shadow
slices the window. Whose
is the other face in the glass? Whose will be
the last face I see? You
look at me. Calculate
in hours
the years between
the decay of flesh and hair, a moment to ponder
that first frozen season,
that bursting room
where three dreams turned and met.

Crimes of the Imagination

Watching your face dissolve into watching me searching
my mirror for a sign, alive
inside the question remembering
in different directions — night birds help keep the wound awake — you
keep a cold fire to simmer the buried insult. I swim the wound
we drowned in again (a swallow
locates itself in the wind).

You say to my hair in the mirror in a ticking voice, "You
are a drop of fire slicing down my spine. " Trying
to swallow your voice while it slashes my face
your bones shine in my skin. You wanted

a son to repeat your face like a robin. When
I'm an old woman with a face like a hawk I'll walk with a cane
carved with a hidden compartment for whiskey.

You're guilty, finally, of crimes of the imagination.
I'm guilty of knowing
that nothing but murder will heal us now.

A few things now

A few things now
don't make me think of you but the night does,
the night's sad perfume. One long night together,
we said, in that room; time enough to memorize our bodies
as they turn and burn and blur, curved in
the world's arm, your thin hands, my legs
around your hips like a dance, the cracked lips and night
tightening
around us.

You could make me sleep you said. No more
white nights. Sink me ripe into sleep, the world
would fold around us like a bed of deep woods. Remember
the words we said? That sentence wormed with light?
How we'd lie together one long fragrant night? Only the two of us

left in the world in the night
love comes back like a lie.

That winter

I began
to read words backwards
shake out my hair and walk in the dark in the house
hollow-handed. Always cutting my fingers, bleeding from the fingers, legs
a puzzle of bruises
walking
into fishtanks, spiderplants, swinging birds — things that look
like other things more than themselves

ironing board up since May at midnight
soaking up death in small doses
walking
and thinking (the house smelled of winter) that

    even you
    with your grief with your arm over me,
    you
    sinking into a beveled edge of me
    carved with the earth's curve plant yourself
    gently
    remembering
    to grow (in code)
    in season I
    felt the sun rub along earth's naked spine, ancient

    light wound around wine shines the bottle and in the belly heat
    shoots straight to the brain, benign
    as forest fire
            waiting

something whistling in the throat
felt his body knot and shoot in opposite directions, lurching dark
stars apart burst past the reptile brain, swallowing light
moon-scarred
into the earth's curve

hers
lying in their separate ways (All over town they're calling
                    to verify my lies.)

something whispers in my throat
a bracelet of dry grass slides past a white skinny wrist
moon cracks apart through cracked glass, a bone
rattles
inside my hand the brain that beats my heart remembers
you.

Still Life

Missed you
in rock time
a long time
past winter. In your absence

I practice
the syntax of silence
so long uninhabited
writing on air in the dark
a Genesis day
to see how it fits
when you're gone, you stand
silent as snow dreams, peaches
in silver bowls
in a Dutch kitchen. Such

a long time this clings
like the odor of old winter, spring
brings to cold bloom
your death
to life.

Morning you came to my room

Morning you came to my room in the rain.
Kissed my wrist, the scar
on my breast.

    Breathe in fire
    Breathe in water
    Breathing slow in a broken place.

Inhale your skin into my skin your voice
walked the bones of my face.

    Move to the music
    Under water

Your face a fire of every color

    A poem humming
    Stumbling sun
    Under your body
    Hands beneath me. Loved me long

as morning lasted. Night
I lost interest in my fate.

Year you tore a path through my brain.
Each surrender more resistless
Scar in the lip that never lifts.

Life forsake me if ever I grieve you, if ever
if ever I forget

    What you were and who can name it.
    What I forgave for your grief.

III.

Threading the Needle

"To live in the past is easy. To live in the present is like threading a needle."

Walker Percy

"We're all scared to death. What you do is you just keep laughing."

Jim Rockford

Squash

We all hated spinach and broccoli and Brussels sprouts but
only Julie hated squash but she hated it enough for all of us but
we didn't feel sorry for her because we could all stand it
with gobs of butter and salt even my little brother Craig
who hated all vegetables and had to stay at the table
about three nights a week till he cleaned his plate but Julie
didn't even butter her squash when it was hot she pushed it
way back on her plate in a leprous blob so none of it touched
her fried chicken and mashed potatoes and dinner roll and finally
my mother, who was raised on vegetables and even liked okra,
would butter it for her but by then it was cold and the butter
just sat there solid as a glob of snot and by then we were done eating
but dragged out dessert to see what Julie would do this time
and she whined and squirmed and claimed her stomach hurt and we
snickered and smirked and lit into our lemon meringue pie,
Julie's favorite, and she held her breath and plugged her nose and
slid a sliver of squash about as big as a gnat's knee through her teeth
and screwed up her face and said "two more bites?" and Mom said
"That was no bite, you eat it all," and Craig hissed "I'll eat it
for a dollar," but that was two weeks' allowance and Julie
never had a nickel she spent it all on Nut Goodies and had had
3 or 4 before supper and hid the wrappers and Dad said "Eat half
of it and you can have your pie," he didn't like squash either
so she squeezed her eyes shut and pinched her nose together and
threw in 2 giant bites and gagged and grabbed her neck and
gushed up squash and mashed potatoes and fried chicken and Nut Goodies
and chunks of dinner roll all over her plate and sprayed the salt and pepper shakers
and the outside napkin in the napkin holder and the edge
of *Portals of Prayer* and Diane and I grabbed our throats
and moaned "OOOoohhh!" and "Uuuggghhhh!" and Mom laid her hand
on Julie's forehead and Dad shook his head and went into the
living room to listen to the Twins and Craig said "Make her eat it
again."

Explaining my father to my brother

My lover talks in a ticking voice about his father, who
beat him,
his son, whom he beat, who died
beneath a car, at nine,
before he could stop.

My father loved his father too,
who neighbors called to kill mad dogs, to pull
feet first, the bloody calves from breeching cows,
to dehorn bulls. Who laughed at his son, my father,
who couldn't wring a chicken's neck: "What kind of farmer
will you make?"

My brother wouldn't play basketball, at six foot four.
Wouldn't take the .22 my father saved for him. His father
is afraid for him.
They seldom speak.

Driving

The radio says a woman is dead. A blow to the head in a hotel room.
Naked. A necklace of fingertip bruises.

Two girls murdered at the county fair. Another year. Their girlfriends look up
'statutory rape' in the *American Heritage Dictionary*.

Four-year-olds pointing to places on dolls their fathers and brothers
have touched them. Their mothers' eyes are broken eggs.

Young mother, eyes set straight in her face. Her eardrum slapped apart
one night. "You're sure a man's hand did that?" the doctor says.

Father, then step-father. One was mean, one wept. Melody
doing the take-away tables with blood between her legs. "Isn't she young
to be menstruating?" the school nurse asks the principal.

Four girls at the light, gravely waiting. Morning faces. Their thin arms.
Thready legs. Point their toes before they go, gallantly along the way.

Homecoming queen in a hotel room. Empty bottle on the floor. Her lover
gone home for the holiday.

Woman who wove beads into her blouse. Sewed bells in the hem of her skirt.
"Turned out he wanted a younger woman. That's why he hit me. Split my lip."

Always shaved a year off her age. Dated her letters one day back. Always
behaved like a great beauty. "After the surgery he wouldn't look at me.
I couldn't blame him. It wasn't pretty."

Hairdresser tells her friend, between perms, how she gagged and threw up
on his hairy belly — how he slapped her out of bed with a crack
upside her head.

Woman who studies the hand of the sleeping man. Eyes full of buried murder
as the ground of this land.

Forced the door. A man she wouldn't go out with anymore. Razor hand
around her throat. "One more time whore — just one more."

Porn queen forced to go down on his friends, his father, strangers
with stabbing faces. Men who could do things for them.

Studying sirens in the night. Beautiful by starts, in certain light.
Eyes like cat eyes caught in the headlights.

"This is funny. This is unusual. A woman don't jump. She'll usually take pills."

(Dip a finger in her blood. Write her name on her forehead.)

Long waisted woman with rocks in her pockets and cold riverwater.
Life runs out like water. Woman who lived as long as she could.

Woman in a witty hat. Woman who could not forget. Her shapely shoulders.
Musical name. Body opens in a yawn. Groans like the grave and takes him in.

Woman taken in fortunetelling. Dreaming of women whose arms end in
stars. "Do you notice how they are always preparing murder for us? "

"Strapped me to the table. The room didn't have a door. White table.
White people. My ears itched something fierce. And then a fire
smeared my brain. 'A little pain to erase the pain. And memory. ' "

Woman in a battered hat. Woman who refused to wait. Stutters
down an empty street. The moon is loose again in her eyelid.

A man in the next car points a gun at my head.
(The radio says a woman is dead.) It's time I learned
to breathe through blood.

Val

That dumb cunt left me off here. I don't know where I am.
I'm going to my daughter's over north. She looks just like me
only pretty. All my girls work — all married to men who work.
I've got enough grandsons but one for a ball team. Eight boys
and a girl. Pearl. After my mother. That's an old name. Nobody
names their girls Pearl anymore.

I was married. He told me what to do every morning before
he went to work — like I was a kid. Told me to upholster an old
easy chair one day and I told him to get fucked and he pitched
a tack hammer at my head and missed and I haven't seen him since.
22 years. He lives south I think. Jackie Welch. He was a good-looking
sonuvabitch.

Does your sister look like you? Three dead in my family since July.
Two the same month. That's why I'm drinking. My baby from crib death
and my brother from a hit and run up by Ely. Drove off and left him
bleeding like a dog in the road. They don't know how long
it took him to die. Bastard was dead drunk. He hit another guy
last fourth of July and he's still on the loose. He won't do no time
for this one neither. He's the sheriff's nephew or something up there.
I marched at the Capitol yesterday. Carried a candle. Mothers after
drunk drivers. Sisters. Don't make no difference.

3:15. Is that clock right? Is that morning or afternoon? Why
is all this shit still up? Isn't Christmas finished yet?

Finnish. I'm a Finlander. Chippewa on my mother's side.
I just got out of Shakopee but don't be scared. I never hurt
nobody but myself.

I don't believe you got a sister over here. You're just saying that
to make me feel better. This is way out of your way, right?

That's the funeral home they was all buried from on the corner up here.
Perlman Brothers. My mother, then my little girl, then Will.

I threw him a party on his birthday last December — at the plant.
Ice cream and cake and the works. Hired a girl to come in
in a fur coat and high heels with nothing on underneath — right
on the line. He was red as his hunting shirt all day. God
he was a sweet guy.

The poet says grief

The poet says grief
never leaves only changes, it
waits outside doors keeps a place
at the table. Hides in a high room
with mirrors to the wall, flings
from the attic to the roof of the mouth.
Whispers at windows.
Slips out with the smoke.
Creeps eave to eave like a grin.

Gathers with night in the trees when we
won't let it in.

I was your first cradle

grave child
and I rocked you down the walk with a book
to the edge of town
down the gravel river
spring and summer over treebones locked
the broken door reading I am a chapel
in the bone and ivory graveyard heard
you tickticking steady as gravity breathing
we breathed together
slept at the same time a hand knit a cradle, knit into a cradle a tomb
of secrets slept through autumn
perfect pocket
secret
as knit roots as
insects pressed between the leaves of ancient books,
safe
inside the world-containing word   small
bones of the wrist collect
behind flesh flash
secret as molebones:
at one we wandered awake
nightwalking
going to see the elephant
going
to live with the crone in the savage chapel balanced on a blade of grass
both of us barefoot;
I was the lady they sawed in half one fainting morning after
I was made wood
matchless
translated
antic
with a flat thin face
without pockets,
I was Thumbelina
courted by the mole
wandering in an unfinished childhood
wandering
then winter tightened on us and I rocked you rocked
rocked you in the black oak rocker.

In the garden

Stunk of fear dumb death
hooted under a rhubarb leaf like a lost goose, you
scooped it up, eyes with sudden time behind them,
child in a room with a corpse
twitching blood from a flowering throat; honked
like a dog with a bone in its throat,
cat-mangled string-dangled
foot.

Wind shook us weak shook us still in the garden,
a flea hopped on your arm, life
soaked back in the ground. "Remember?"
"the sparrow we saved?" you said later, "from the gray cat?"
"What sparrow was that?"
"*You* know. We kept it in a box in the kitchen.
Under the window. You couldn't wait till I got home
from kindergarden one day. You let it go without me.
I was mad all afternoon."

Dad told me Grandpa, who neighbors called to kill mad dogs,
when he had one himself, not mad but crazy after heifers' tails,
bit them off to bloody stumps, shot her
so it wouldn't show, chopped a half-grown birch and laid it on her,
but dad wasn't fooled, or his sisters, but pretended they were.

"I guess," say Garret, "this rabbit won't be so lucky."

This kitten will outlive me

walking the length of my bath,
taking my measure with grave kitten symmetry waiting
for white islands cat-dangles
one paw, shakes it
as if
shaking off fire.

She wants to walk on water.

I slap water at her, all laid out, her
ears fold back, a collection of dying parts
swims in her drowning eyes
something shining
under the water, crouches
as if she will interrupt
the mad-red spot
under the water, I grab for her foot, she cat-dances
high-backed turns on a drop licks her foot. Her throat
cat-rattles, I riddle
my fingers into my hair and wait, braided
under the plushy water, her paw
silks the loosening skin of my wrist. We look
for a sign under the skin.

I should line up some land for her to land on.
Should do something Roman — I grab for her rabbit's foot. She watches
my eyes, I raise
one luminous knee
                    (If thy breast offend thee
                    If death offend thee)

This life
These lives
have come
through millions of deaths
I say to this kitten
baptized
into my bath.

Step lovely.

Lump

Unspoken lump
muscleless whisper,
secret as molebones, slow
fish to the heart
or lightning in a high drawer clenched
in a crescent
box at the back.

Making a place for itself for
the place
I didn't make.

Another footprint on the heart,
Crusoe on the beach.

You sent me a poem

about a woman you love,
married
graceful
with brittle wit and a fat-ankled baby.
I am not graceful   no longer
married   my fingers tick
on the book you sent me

my son is taller than you by six inches
and brown as fall and full of fawn-legged grace.

I always look just awakened
you say
"I flamed in your mad-red hair a day
before we burned out"
in your braided fingers, our lives
have been much-interlaced. Tell me,

do you have a poem for me?

Having been lost

"Try to be one of those people on whom nothing is lost."
Henry James

Having been lost on every man I've ever known save one,
and him gone, I turn to you in the dissolving dark,
your slender fingers, tender neck, old ache
in the unmending throat, old friend, whose nimble mind fits
my wit like a thimble:

These things: How we finished each other's puns and allusions;
knew all the same books, jokes, poems, stories
unspooled, morning to evening, before we were
each other's secret. The trees and the birdsongs
you gave me, later, the letters, our journals,
feathered together. New York. The pictures
we took in the park, setting the timer and rushing
together. Only our skin held us in.

Pictured ourselves in Amalfi in winter, laughing
in broken Italian. You said we could sail in my body a year
and a day. We hold that note a moment. A planet unravels. Said I was
the true seamless wife of your brain and soul, old ache, our breath
threads together. Said we couldn't live in a poem forever, old friend,
about to be gone.

So I mourn on the page, say, at the same time (I zip up my wit,
move to another room): This split fits in my cupboard of loss
like a cup, last of a set. Makes a pattern my soul can't resist.

Now we're stitched into paradox, last in Pandora's box.

You said we could sail on the silk of my body. I thought
it was only your brain I believed in so why do I blossom
where your hand has been?

Personals

Looking for a man
who doesn't know his sign or resting heart rate;
who only runs to catch a bus; can't tell sushi
from raw fish. Thinks Zinfandel is the guy
who used to star in *The FBI*. Has no VCR, PC,
IRA, BMW. No vanity plates or gifted kids. No cat
named after a literary figure. No whimsical furniture,
Calvin underwear, Armani suit or silent quartz movement Rolex
that beeps on the hour. Doesn't sleep too well
or smell like Perry Ellis. Completely ignores
at least two of the basic food groups. Can't remember jokes —
makes up his own. Doesn't make me talk to his machine.
Never phones me from a tanning booth, sensory deprivation tank,
his briefcase, ex-wife's condo, a moving vehicle. Always
asks the right questions. Never tries to cheer me up
when I'm sentimentally depressed.
Doesn't get a hard-on thinking
about compound interest. Doesn't count my drinks
or try to improve my character
Has no discernible lifestyle.

Ok, 8

(after listening to Mpls. poets read their poems on the radio)

They're all writing poems full of names — placenames
street names freeways cafes store names
brand names for God's sake! It's not a poem
it seems unless it's got I-94 or the Rainbow Cafe stuck in it,
or Kit-Kat candy.

I'm all for names (been looking forever for a poem for Odor-O-No) but
I've spent half my life in this city and can't think of 3 places
I'd put in a poem.

There's the old Mixers on 7 Corners before it turned candy-assed and expensive
(Sergeant Preston's, if you please), and Hennepin Methodist Church
which even the 35W offramp slicing across its breathless steeple can't wreck
completely.

Maybe a couple of houses whose addresses I don't know anymore and
wouldn't name a poem after if I did except maybe 2509 3rd Ave. So.,
Ann Sothern's old house the landlord told me once, she was a girl there
where my marriage broke up and down where I lived
for $115 a month, utilities included, 10 years ago 3 floors 4 bedrooms 2
lace-iron fireplaces, wainscot walls oak woodwork to break your heart so
deep and dark till they knocked it down to make a parking lot for the
Art Institute.

I might name a poem "2509 3rd Ave. So."

Or Humphrey's grave (ok 4), 36th & Emerson when snow ghosts roost in the
evergreens and they put out the hundred wreaths, anonymous as grass.

And dozens of trees. Sometimes I say trees the way Nick Adams said names —
everyone he'd ever known, by rote, at night, and railroad stops when that ran out
to get to sleep, beginning with the cottonwood Grandpa chopped to make more cornfield
and didn't know why I wouldn't look at him all afternoon. I start with that
but end up in the city since I've lived here too long
not to have loved some city trees — end with the great cavey 3-trunked oak by the
trash cans behind my apartment at 3446 Colfax that's the best thing about 3446

and why I live here. Skinny-armed pine forever dying, Garfield & 34th, fall-yellow
bog larch, bark rough as carp, Lake and Girard and another oak, old as Blake's oak
and black, 90 years closer to heaven than I will ever be, Pillsbury at 39th;
tall bony elm sighed in windstorms on Emerson, sumac and smokebush around it
a storm of mushroom spores under it; flowering dogwood the white squirrel lived in,
36th & Elliot and working back, Ann Sothern's purple plums. I wrote a poem
about the Lyndale trees the tornado broke 2 Junes ago and sent it to the *Lake St.
Review* but they didn't print it and I lost faith, but not in trees. Maybe
I should have put in their addresses — red crossed-elm, 3711 Lyndale; 4318 evergreen —
their names.

Maybe you have to come from Brooklyn or Boston or be born here to care about
this city.

Maybe the spot at the damned Institute where the Chinese poets stroll
around the jade mountain, 2nd floor north, or the Rare Books Room at Wilson
or Market Bar-B-Q, 1st & Glenwood downtown or the old Nankin.

Or that aching spot on Cedar Lake.

Ok, 8.